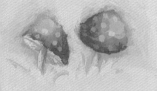

Abigail and Benjamin Falconer –
wishing you both lots of wonderful adventures.
With love, Auntie Pam

To Nige – this is for you.
All my love, B xxx

First published 2007 by Macmillan Children's Books
a division of Macmillan Publishers Limited
20 New Wharf Road, London N1 9RR
Basingstoke and Oxford
Associated companies worldwide
www.panmacmillan.com

ISBN: 978-0-333-99048-3 (HB)
ISBN: 978-0-333-99049-0 (PB)

Text copyright © Pamela Duncan Edwards 2007
Illustrations copyright © Rebecca Harry 2007
Moral rights asserted.

1 3 5 7 9 8 6 4 2

A CIP catalogue record for this book is available from the British Library.

Printed in Belgium

I'm BIG Enough Now!

Written by Pamela Duncan Edwards

Illustrated by Rebecca Harry

MACMILLAN CHILDREN'S BOOKS

One day there was a baby elephant who said, "I want to go and have adventures by myself. I'm big enough now!"

"Are you sure?" asked her big, wise elephant mum.

"If I were you, I'd wait until I'd grown up some more."

The baby elephant stamped her feet.
"I don't want to wait. I want to go today!"
"Okay," said her big, wise mum. "Where are you going first?"
"To the lake," said the baby elephant. "I'm big enough now!"

And off she went.

The baby elephant paddled in the water.
"This is a good adventure!" she laughed.

But then a gigantic old hippopotamus
made a splishy-splashy wave.
"Help!" spluttered the baby elephant.
"This water's too deep."

"Why, hello!" said a soft, kind voice.
"I was just passing. Catch hold of my trunk."
The baby elephant's big, wise mum patted her gently.
"There, there," she said. "No harm done. Now where
are you going next?"

"To the village," said the baby elephant.
"I'm big enough now!"

And off she went.

"This is a great adventure!" laughed the baby elephant,
as she chased a piece of paper down the dusty street.

But then she heard clackety voices, floppety feet and honkety horns. "It's too noisy!" she whimpered.

"Why, it's you again!" said a soft, kind voice. "I was just passing."
The baby elephant's big, wise mum gave her a huge kiss.
  "There, there," she said. "No harm done.
  So where are you going next?"

"To the jungle," said the baby elephant.
"I'm big enough now!"

And off she went.

"This is an excellent adventure!"
laughed the baby elephant, as she marched
through the thick leaves.

But suddenly, around the corner,
came a squeaky, scary . . .

MONSTER!

"I want my mum!" wailed the baby elephant.
And she began to cry.

"Here I am!" said a soft, kind voice.

The squeaky, scary monster ran away.

"Now," said the baby elephant's big, wise mum, "I'm off to have some adventures too. Do you want to come with me?"
"Okay," said the baby elephant.

And off they went together.

They went to the lake and squirted the gigantic
old hippopotamus until he laughed and laughed.

They went to the village and had buns and bananas.

They skipped through the jungle,

they played chase with the parrots,

and they danced with the monkeys.

At bedtime they sang to the moon
and waved to the stars.

"I liked my adventures with you,"
said the baby elephant.
"So when are you going off on your own
again?" asked her big, wise mum.

The baby elephant
thought for a minute.

"I think I'm going to wait,"
she said. "I'm not big enough yet!"

Her mum hugged her tight.
"You soon will be," she said,
"my little, wise baby elephant."